LIFE

BRAVING ADULTHOOD WITH BIBLICAL PASSION

QUEST

CARY SCHMIDT

First published in 2011 by Striving Together Publications, a ministry of Lancaster Baptist Church, Lancaster, CA 93535. Striving Together Publications is committed to providing tried, trusted, and proven books that will further equip local churches to carry out the Great Commission. Your comments and suggestions are valued.

Striving Together Publications
4020 E. Lancaster Blvd.
Lancaster, CA 93535
800.201.7748

Cover design by Jeremy Lofgren
Layout by Craig Parker
Edited by Amanda Michael, Sarah Michael, and Danielle Mordh
Special thanks to our proofreaders.

ISBN 978-1-59894-113-5

Printed in the United States of America

Table of Contents

I Want To Be Four Again
The Root Causes of Refusing to Grow Up

Text
1 CORINTHIANS 13:11

11 *When I was a child, I spake as a child, I understood as a child, I thought as a child: but when I became a man, I put away childish things.*

Overview
The first few lessons of this study focus on "What's holding us back?"—identifying the things that draw us into problems and prevent our lives from being blessed and abundant as God designed. These are the things that keep us from going forward in life.

This first lesson pulls material from both the introduction and chapter 1 of *Life Quest*, and it introduces the problems of present day young adult culture. The message of the past couple of generations has given young adults of the present little motivation to embrace the maturity and responsibility of courageous adulthood. This lesson challenges the student to embrace both maturity and responsibility.

Lesson Aim
To introduce two key words of successful adult life—maturity and responsibility, and why they matter. To begin helping students understand that maturity and responsibility are both blessed in adult life.

Introduction

_____

_____

_____

I. Understanding the Collective

_____

A. We've taken away your _____.

B. We've told you that you _____ from nothing.

C. We've shown you horrific examples of _____ and _____.

D. We've taught you that sex can be with anyone at any time for any reason—_____.

E. We've become disillusioned with our _____ and _____.

F. We've taught you that life is about _____.

G. We've taught you to take the path of least _____.

PSALM 146:5
5   _Happy is he that hath the God of Jacob for his help, whose hope is in the LORD his God._

II. _____
—To Be or Not to Be?

A. Immaturity seeks _____; maturity seeks
   _____.

B. Immaturity seeks _____; maturity
   seeks _____.

C. Immaturity seeks _____; maturity
   seeks _____.

D. Immaturity seeks immediate _____;
   maturity seeks long-term _____.

E. Immaturity seeks _____; maturity seeks
   _____.

Conclusion

_____

_____

_____

Study Questions

1. How has culture attacked your faith and tried to shake your belief in God?

2. What mistakes or dynamics have you seen in the lives of others that cause you to be more fearful of your future?

3. In what ways do you feel you are unprepared for a successful adulthood?

4. What responsibilities has God placed in your life that are not really "fun"?

5. List some of the prices you would pay if you failed to embrace responsibility as God would have you to.

6. List four areas in which culture provides a path of immediate gratification when God says to wait for long-term blessings.

7.	Grade yourself on the five comparisons between immaturity and maturity.

8.	Take a moment in prayer right now and make a covenant with God that you will embrace maturity and responsibility as He leads you. Choose, with Moses, to endure by God's grace rather than to enjoy the pleasures of sin.

Memory Verse

"Being confident of this very thing, that he which hath begun a good work in you will perform it until the day of Jesus Christ:"
—PHILIPPIANS 1:6

Live Stupid, Die Young

Overcoming Ignorance and Rebellion

Text

PROVERBS 1:1–5

1   *The proverbs of Solomon the son of David, king of Israel;*

2   *To know wisdom and instruction; to perceive the words of understanding;*

3   *To receive the instruction of wisdom, justice, and judgment, and equity;*

4   *To give subtilty to the simple, to the young man knowledge and discretion.*

5   *A wise man will hear, and will increase learning; and a man of understanding shall attain unto wise counsels:*

Overview

Focusing on "What's holding us back?"—this lesson connects a rebellious life to an ignorant life, and explains how rebellion against God's principles just amounts to stupidity. It introduces the four kinds of people found in the book of Proverbs—the wise, the simple, the fool, the scorner—and profiles each. By the end of the lesson, hopefully students will find the life and profile of a wise man attractive, and will be able to identify traces of the other three types of people in their own character as God reveals it. The student should see the contrast that, though culture teaches them and expects them to be foolish, God desires to make them wise.

Lesson Aim

To draw the students toward the pursuit of God's wisdom and away from the simplicity, foolishness, or scorn that is so common in today's secular culture.

Introduction

_____

_____

_____

I. Look Who's Calling You _____

_____

_____

II. How _____ and _____ Go Together

_____

_____

III. The Four _____-_____ of Proverbs

A. The _____

B. The _____

C. The _____

D. The _____

Conclusion

_____

_____

Study Questions

1. List a couple of times that unsaved people have tried to make you feel stupid for your faith or biblical convictions.

2. Describe some ways you've recently seen people do spiritually harmful things to their lives.

3. In what ways does your life exhibit the qualities of a wise person?

4. In what ways does your life exhibit the qualities of a simple person, a fool, or a scorner?

5. Define the word *scorner* from this lesson.

6. Read the first chapter of Proverbs and write down as many character traits of a wise person as you can find.

7. Write out James 1:5.

8. Briefly write out how God would have you respond to the four types of people we studied. What should your relationship be with each of the four? (Wise, simple, fool, scorner)

Memory Verses

"If any of you lack wisdom, let him ask of God, that giveth to all men liberally, and upbraideth not; and it shall be given him."
—JAMES 1:5

A Lesson Even a Dog Can Learn
Overcoming Folly

Text

ECCLESIASTES 1:17

17 And I gave my heart to know wisdom, and to know madness and folly: I perceived that this also is vexation of spirit.

Overview

Continuing to focus on "What's holding us back?"—this lesson focuses in on the key problem for simple people, fools, and scorners—the primary word the Bible uses is *folly*. The lesson defines folly and then helps the student identify modern day folly. Anything that detours us from biblical principles and a life lived in God's will adds up to folly. The lesson explores what God's Word says about folly, and then more closely examines four common types of folly found in young adults—distraction, selfish desires, fear, and bitterness.

Distraction is anything that consumes my time to the point that I am not pursuing God's purpose and plan. Selfish desires are those fleshly desires that would tempt me to break God's laws and live in sin. Fear is that hesitation to take risks, express faith, and live courageously for God. Bitterness is allowing past hurts or the failures of others to play into present day decisions to the point that I miss out on God's best.

Lesson Aim

To help students understand what folly looks like in their own lives, and then to deliberately choose a life that avoids folly and pursues God's will.

Introduction

_____

_____

_____

I. _____ **Folly**

_____

_____

_____

II. _____ **Is Folly**

_____

_____

_____

III. _____ **Are Folly**

_____

_____

_____

IV. _____ **Is Folly**

_____

_____

_____

V. _____ **Is Folly**

A. Follow _____ with all men.

B. Diligently choose God's _____.

C. Keep choosing God's _____ for the rest of your life.

Conclusion

_____

_____

_____

Study Questions

1.   How does God describe and define folly in His Word?

2.   List the four major areas of folly that young adults today are facing.

3.   List the things that Satan will try to use in your life to draw you off of God's course. (This is your folly.)

4.   List the things that you are the most afraid of as you consider your future.

5.   List the selfish desires that might become folly in your life.

6.   List a few ways that you have been hurt in the past and who hurt you.

7.   Describe what you will do with the hurt listed above.

8. Spend a moment in prayer about the four areas of folly that we've studied. Ask the Lord to expose areas in your life where you may get ensnared in folly, and ask for His guidance and protection.

Memory Verses

"Then I saw that wisdom excelleth folly, as far as light excelleth darkness."—ECCLESIASTES 2:13

A Man Can't Just Sit Around
Reward #1—A Life of Eternal Significance

Text

JEREMIAH 24:5–7

5 *Thus saith the LORD, the God of Israel; Like these good figs, so will I acknowledge them that are carried away captive of Judah, whom I have sent out of this place into the land of the Chaldeans for their good.*

6 *For I will set mine eyes upon them for good, and I will bring them again to this land: and I will build them, and not pull them down; and I will plant them, and not pluck them up.*

7 *And I will give them an heart to know me, that I am the LORD: and they shall be my people, and I will be their God: for they shall return unto me with their whole heart.*

Overview

This lesson is based upon chapters 4 and 5 of *Life Quest*, and it turns a corner in the series. The past few lessons have been focused on "What's holding us back?"—identifying the problems of young adult life in culture (ignorance, rebellion, immaturity, folly, etc.). These are the things that hold young adults back from experiencing God's best.

With this lesson we begin to examine the truth of God's Word about "What's waiting for you?" In this section of the study we will closely examine four great blessings of embracing adulthood with courage and commitment. The first great reward is a life of eternal significance. The lesson challenges students that a life well lived results in a life that matters eternally—this is the deepest desire of every heart, to know that our lives really matter.

Lesson Aim

To help the students understand the blessing of a life lived for God and to see the reward of a life of eternal value.

Introduction

_____

_____

_____

I. You Matter to _____

_____

_____

_____

JEREMIAH 24:5–7

5   Thus saith the LORD, the God of Israel; Like these good figs, so will I acknowledge them that are carried away captive of Judah, whom I have sent out of this place into the land of the Chaldeans for their good.

6   For I will set mine eyes upon them for good, and I will bring them again to this land: and I will build them, and not pull them down; and I will plant them, and not pluck them up.

7   And I will give them an heart to know me, that I am the LORD: and they shall be my people, and I will be their God: for they shall return unto me with their whole heart.

JEREMIAH 29:10–13

10   For thus saith the LORD, That after seventy years be accomplished at Babylon I will visit you, and perform my good word toward you, in causing you to return to this place.

11   For I know the thoughts that I think toward you, saith the LORD, thoughts of peace, and not of evil, to give you an expected end.

12   Then shall ye call upon me, and ye shall go and pray unto me, and I will hearken unto you.

13   And ye shall seek me, and find me, when ye shall search for me with all your heart.

A. God _____ of you.

B. God _____ _____ of you.

C. God has developed an _____ plan for your life.

II. You Matter to _____

_____

_____

_____

III. Life Will Drop You _____, but God

_____

_____

_____

_____

Conclusion

_____

_____

_____

Study Questions

1. List three things that are commonly "holding us back" from growing into successful adult lives.

2. Write out Ephesians 5:14 and describe how this verse applies to your life right now.

3. Describe in a paragraph the "why" of your life. Why do you live each day, work, etc.?

4. Read Jeremiah 24 and describe what God teaches you from this chapter.

5. List the people your life matters to—the people you influence—right now.

6. List the people in your future, perhaps those you don't even know yet, who will be impacted by your choices.

7. What has God given you to do today that you should embrace and pursue passionately?

8. In what ways can you redeem some time and invest your life this week? What will you not do? What will you do instead?

Memory Verse

"Thou wilt shew me the path of life: in thy presence is fulness of joy; at thy right hand there are pleasures for evermore."
—PSALM 16:11

When Big Things Mean Nothing, and Everything Means Something

Reward #2—The Timeless Gifts of a Good Life

Text

JAMES 1:17

17 Every good gift and every perfect gift is from above, and cometh down from the Father of lights, with whom is no variableness, neither shadow of turning.

Overview

The first reward of a passionate adult life is a life of eternal significance. The second reward is a life that experiences the good gifts of God every day, in small and big ways. This lesson explores the good blessings of God that come with a life lived within His purposes.

Every young adult hopes for a good life, but few of them realize that their choices and direction are often preventing the best blessings of life. This lesson helps the student to see God as the ultimate gift-giver. His heart is overwhelmingly good, and His unfolding plans for our lives include a multitude of good gifts that we would otherwise never enjoy.

Lesson Aim

To help students see that countless gifts from the gracious hand of God are awaiting them if they will seize God's purpose for their adult lives and live today in His perfect will.

Introduction

_____

_____

_____

I. The _____ Gifts of a Good Life

A. God _____ in giving good gifts to His children.

B. God's _____ gifts are _____.

C. God's gifts follow _____ and _____.

D. God will be _____ to you than you could be to _____!

II. God's _____ Hold the Most _____

A. When _____ are your own giver, things mean _____.

B. When _____ is the giver, everything means something _____!

Conclusion

_____

_____

_____

Study Questions

1. Write out Psalm 84:11 and think about it's message to you.

2. Write a paragraph describing the heart of God that was studied in this lesson.

3. Describe why God takes us through pressure or difficulty.

4. According to Philippians 4:19, how does God promise to meet our needs?

5. List three small things in your life that hold great significance because of who gave them to you.

6. Describe two or three things in life that you appreciate less because you gave them to yourself.

7. According to the end of this lesson, what does God specialize in?

8. Describe your thoughts and emotions when considering "surrendering to God's perfect will."

Memory Verse

"But as it is written, Eye hath not seen, nor ear heard, neither have entered into the heart of man, the things which God hath prepared for them that love him."—1 CORINTHIANS 2:9

One Red Paper Clip, Please

Reward #3—The Eternal Rewards of
a Faithful Steward

Text

1 CORINTHIANS 6:19–20

19 What? know ye not that your body is the temple of the Holy Ghost which is in you, which ye have of God, and ye are not your own?

20 For ye are bought with a price: therefore glorify God in your body, and in your spirit, which are God's.

Overview

The first two rewards of a well-lived life—a life of eternal significance and the timeless gifts of a good life, lead to a third and final compelling reward—the eternal reward of a faithful steward. There's something incredible about knowing you are living your life in a way that pleases God and stewards the things He has given to you. Everyone is headed to accountability to the Lord. Each Christian will answer to God for what they did with their life.

This lesson focuses on the stewardship of life and the eternal reward of pleasing God and hearing, "Well done." It focuses the student on the eternal and on living a life that will endure the test of time.

Lesson Aim

To help the students understand and embrace accountability before God and the stewardship of life for eternal purposes.

Introduction

_____

_____

_____

I. _____ Isn't the Cure All

_____

_____

_____

II. God's Excessive _____ Just Keeps on Going

EPHESIANS 2:4–7

4   But God, who is rich in mercy, for his great love wherewith he loved us,

5   Even when we were dead in sins, hath quickened us together with Christ, (by grace ye are saved;)

6   And hath raised us up together, and made us sit together in heavenly places in Christ Jesus:

7   That in the ages to come he might shew the exceeding riches of his grace in his kindness toward us through Christ Jesus.

A. You will anticipate _____.

B. You will get _____ about living life correctly now so that you can _____ God!

III. Jesus Describes the _____ of Life

A. You must _____ your gifts.

B. You must _____ your gifts.

C. You must _____ your gifts.

IV. The Soon-Coming _____ Ceremony

_____

_____

_____

Conclusion

_____

_____

_____

Study Questions

1. Describe the predictable path of disappointment that many people take in life.

2. What two responses will you have when you begin to live life in light of eternity?

3. List three things you could do right now to begin being a better steward of your life.

4. Describe the gifts that God has given to you. Ask others for input on this.

5. For each of the gifts you described above, list one or two things you could begin doing to discover and use your gifts for God.

6. God's Word teaches that every Christian will one day appear before what?

7.   What are some ways that lost people experiment with life only to end up with regret?

8.   Write out the memory verses below and ask the Lord to help you live with eternal rewards in mind.

Memory Verses

"Now if any man build upon this foundation gold, silver, precious stones, wood, hay, stubble; Every man's work shall be made manifest: for the day shall declare it, because it shall be revealed by fire; and the fire shall try every man's work of what sort it is. If any man's work abide which he hath built thereupon, he shall receive a reward."—1 CORINTHIANS 3:12–14

Surf's Up Old Dude
Turning the Corner and Getting on Track

Text

JOSHUA 23:2–3

2   And Joshua called for all Israel, and for their elders, and for their heads, and for their judges, and for their officers, and said unto them, I am old and stricken in age:

3   And ye have seen all that the LORD your God hath done unto all these nations because of you; for the LORD your God is he that hath fought for you.

JOSHUA 23:6–11

6   Be ye therefore very courageous to keep and to do all that is written in the book of the law of Moses, that ye turn not aside therefrom to the right hand or to the left;

7   That ye come not among these nations, these that remain among you; neither make mention of the name of their gods, nor cause to swear by them, neither serve them, nor bow yourselves unto them:

8   But cleave unto the LORD your God, as ye have done unto this day.

9   For the LORD hath driven out from before you great nations and strong: but as for you, no man hath been able to stand before you unto this day.

10   One man of you shall chase a thousand: for the LORD your God, he it is that fighteth for you, as he hath promised you.

11   Take good heed therefore unto yourselves, that ye love the LORD your God.

Overview

This lesson is a pause between parts two and three of this study and is designed to be a review. It's a week to give an overview of the first two parts and see them in "big picture" view. It's a week to pause and discuss what's been studied and how the truth has impacted lives.

The lesson also provides a glimpse into the life of a very courageous Bible character—Joshua, and how he finished his journey.

Lesson Aim

To give a big picture perspective, through the life of Joshua, of the previous six lessons—the things that keep us from moving forward, and the blessings that await us when we move forward.

Introduction

_____

_____

_____

I. Remembering What's _____ Us _____

_____

_____

_____

II. Remembering What's _____ For Us

_____

_____

_____

III. How Joshua Felt about _____ God in Life

_____

_____

_____

JOSHUA 23:2–3, 6–11

2   And Joshua called for all Israel, and for their elders, and for their heads, and for their judges, and for their officers, and said unto them, I am old and stricken in age:

3   And ye have seen all that the LORD your God hath done unto all these nations because of you; for the LORD your God is he that hath fought for you.

6   Be ye therefore very courageous to keep and to do all that is written in the book of the law of Moses, that ye turn not aside therefrom to the right hand or to the left;

7   That ye come not among these nations, these that remain among you; neither make mention of the name of their gods, nor cause to swear by them, neither serve them, nor bow yourselves unto them:

8   But cleave unto the LORD your God, as ye have done unto this day.

9   For the LORD hath driven out from before you great nations and strong: but as for you, no man hath been able to stand before you unto this day.

10   One man of you shall chase a thousand: for the LORD your God, he it is that fighteth for you, as he hath promised you.

11   Take good heed therefore unto yourselves, that ye love the LORD your God.

Conclusion

_____

_____

_____

Study Questions

1. Take a few moments and write down the most critical lessons God has taught you through this study so far.

2. List the four things that hold young adults back from following God with passion.

3. List the three great rewards in store for those who embrace adulthood with biblical passion.

4. Describe in paragraph form what you would like to say about your life once you've reached the end of your journey.

5. List the right decisions that Joshua made that led him to a life without regrets.

6. What things in your life threaten to take the place of God?

7. Write out Joshua 23:8 and 23:11.

8. Write a prayer to God expressing your heart to Him in pressing forward in life.

Memory Verse

"I beseech you therefore, brethren, by the mercies of God, that ye present your bodies a living sacrifice, holy, acceptable unto God, which is your reasonable service. And be not conformed to this world: but be ye transformed by the renewing of your mind, that ye may prove what is that good, and acceptable, and perfect, will of God."—ROMANS 12:1–2

A Passion for God—Part One
Embracing Personal Intimacy with God

Text

REVELATION 3:20

20 Behold, I stand at the door, and knock: if any man hear my voice, and open the door, I will come in to him, and will sup with him, and he with me.

Overview

The first step to embracing adulthood with biblical passion is to embrace a personal, intimate relationship with God. This lesson is the first of a two part lesson about walking with God and developing a personal passion for Him. It breaks down the basics of how any relationship develops— with time that includes communication, consistency, quantity, and continuity. This lesson really focuses on breaking the students out of redundant or impersonal religious practices and helping them develop a dynamic, personal walk with God.

Lesson Aim

To help students understand that walking with God is a personal intimate experience that requires an investment of time and heart.

Introduction

_____

_____

_____

I. A Personal "_____ _____"

_____

_____

_____

II. A Close Relationship Begins by _____

_____

_____

_____

III. A Close Relationship Is _____ but Not _____

_____

_____

_____

IV. A Close Relationship Is _____ through Time

A. Time with God requires _____.

B. Time with God requires _____.

C. Time with God requires _____.

D. Time with God requires _____.

Conclusion

_____

_____

_____

Study Questions

1. Describe the most difficult moment of your life.

2. Describe where you went for help and how you dealt with that difficult situation.

3. Write out Revelation 3:20 and explain how it personally applies to you today.

4. Write a paragraph summarizing the condition of your relationship with God right now.

5. List three things you could do this week to grow and improve your relationship with God.

6. List the first four ways that "time with God" should play out in your life.

7. List the things that are preventing you from spending more time with God.

8. Take a moment and write a prayer to the Lord expressing your heart to know Him more intimately.

Memory Verse

"He giveth power to the faint; and to them that have no might he increaseth strength. Even the youths shall faint and be weary, and the young men shall utterly fall: But they that wait upon the LORD shall renew their strength; they shall mount up with wings as eagles; they shall run, and not be weary; and they shall walk, and not faint."—ISAIAH 40:29–31

A Passion for God—Part Two
Embracing Personal Intimacy with God

Text

JOSHUA 24:15

15 And if it seem evil unto you to serve the LORD, choose you this day whom ye will serve; whether the gods which your fathers served that were on the other side of the flood, or the gods of the Amorites, in whose land ye dwell: but as for me and my house, we will serve the LORD.

Overview

This lesson is part two of a study on developing personal intimacy with God. In this lesson, we will explore five more qualities of a close relationship—transparency, commitment, trust, exclusivity, and submission. Each of these principles explains how a relationship with God can become more intimate and passionate.

This lesson is intended to break preconceived but limited paradigms of walking with God, and reveal how God desires to be our Heavenly Father in a close, personal relationship. Through it, the student should be compelled to develop a vibrant, intimate, daily walk with God.

Lesson Aim

To challenge students to walk personally with God in ways they perhaps haven't considered, and to help them understand that God desires close, personal fellowship with them.

Introduction

_____

_____

_____

GENESIS 39:2
2   And the LORD was with Joseph, and he was a prosperous man....

GENESIS 39:3
3   And his master saw that the LORD was with him, and that the LORD made all that he did to prosper in his hand.

JOSHUA 6:27
27   So the LORD was with Joshua; and his fame was noised throughout all the country.

1 SAMUEL 3:19
19   And Samuel grew, and the LORD was with him, and did let none of his words fall to the ground.

1 SAMUEL 18:12
12   And Saul was afraid of David, because the LORD was with him, and was departed from Saul.

MATTHEW 1:23
23   Behold, a virgin shall be with child, and shall bring forth a son, and they shall call his name Emmanuel, which being interpreted is, God with us.

I. A Close Relationship Requires _____

_____

_____

_____

II. A Close Relationship _____ through _____

_____

_____

_____

III. A Close Relationship _____ through _____

_____

_____

_____

IV. A Close Relationship Becomes _____ through _____

_____

_____

_____

V. A Close Relationship _____ on _____

_____

_____

_____

Conclusion

_____

_____

_____

Study Questions

1. Describe what it means to be transparent with God.

2. What happens to any relationship in life that is begun with a "try it and see" mentality?

3. What does God desire for you to fully commit to, and what's holding you back?

4. When you consider God's will versus your own plans, what scares you the most?

5. What things in your life most threaten God's place of exclusivity?

6. Describe one time in your life when you submitted to God and He blessed you as a result.

7. In what areas of your life do you really need God's help right now?

8. Take a moment and speak to God about the areas you listed in number seven.

Memory Verse

"Wherefore be ye not unwise, but understanding what the will of the Lord is."—EPHESIANS 5:17

A Passion for God's Perfect Will—Part One

Embracing God's Purpose

Text

2 CORINTHIANS 10:5

5   Casting down imaginations, and every high thing that exalteth itself against the knowledge of God, and bringing into captivity every thought to the obedience of Christ;

1 CORINTHIANS 2:9

9   But as it is written, Eye hath not seen, nor ear heard, neither have entered into the heart of man, the things which God hath prepared for them that love him.

Overview

This lesson is the first of two that explores a passion for the will of God. To biblically embrace adulthood, we must first be passionate about God, and we must also be passionate about doing His will. This lesson contrasts our imagination with God's vision. The world attempts to live out their imaginations of a good life, but Christians should seek and pursue the fulfillment of God's vision for their lives.

The focus of the lesson is on helping the students begin to let go of imagination and embrace God's vision for their future. One of the most important aspects of the lesson is how a life calling (from God) already connects to our identity (as designed by God.) In other words, God designed our gifts, abilities, and personality (identity) to match our calling in His will (our purpose in life.) A succinct way to say this is, "God's perfect will is when who you are meets why you are."

Lesson Aim

To help the students begin to capture God's vision for their lives and pursue it with passion.

Introduction

_____

_____

_____

I. God's _____ of My Desires

   A. Desires could be _____ you and setting you up for _____.

   B. Desires will _____.

   C. The best life is when your unique identity meets your life's calling—_____ _____.

II. God's Extravagance vs. My _____ Imagination

_____

_____

_____

III. Commit to God's _____ and _____

_____

_____

_____

IV. Finding Your Way in _____ Will

_____

_____

_____

Conclusion

_____

_____

_____

Study Questions

1. Define the word *identity* and how it applies to you.

2. Define the word *calling* and how it applies to you.

3. Describe how God's vision is different from man's imagination.

4. Why should we distrust our best desires?

5. What do we call the meeting of your unique identity and your God-given calling?

6. What do you believe God is calling you to do next in your life?

7. What could prevent you from doing God's will today?

8. Write out 1 Corinthians 2:9.

Memory Verse

"But without faith it is impossible to please him: for he that cometh to God must believe that he is, and that he is a rewarder of them that diligently seek him."—HEBREWS 11:6

A Passion for God's Perfect Will—Part Two

Embracing God's Purpose

Text

GENESIS 24:12–15

12   And he said, O LORD God of my master Abraham, I pray thee, send me good speed this day, and shew kindness unto my master Abraham.

13   Behold, I stand here by the well of water; and the daughters of the men of the city come out to draw water:

14   And let it come to pass, that the damsel to whom I shall say, Let down thy pitcher, I pray thee, that I may drink; and she shall say, Drink, and I will give thy camels drink also: let the same be she that thou hast appointed for thy servant Isaac; and thereby shall I know that thou hast shewed kindness unto my master.

15   And it came to pass, before he had done speaking, that, behold, Rebekah came out, who was born to Bethuel, son of Milcah, the wife of Nahor, Abraham's brother, with her pitcher upon her shoulder.

Overview

This lesson is part two of the study of developing a passion for God's perfect will. It begins with an exploration of Genesis 24, which you should read. The story of Isaac and Rebekah is a powerful story of how God leads and guides us into His perfect will as we fully trust Him and acknowledge Him.

The lesson has four parts—the story of God's leading in Genesis 24, a few thoughts on developing a biblical process of decision making, principles of how to handle a conflict of wills between you and God, and finally the need for a team of advisors for making big decisions. Each of these parts plays into the whole picture of finding and doing the will of God.

Lesson Aim

To help students understand how to discover and follow the perfect will of God for their futures.

Introduction

_____

_____

_____

ROMANS 8:28

28 And we know that all things work together for good to them that love God, to them who are the called according to his purpose.

I. An Awesome Love Story of God's _____

A. God's will involves being in God's _____.

B. God's will sometimes involves seasons of _____.

C. God's will requires a _____ heart.

II. Establishing a Biblical _____ Process

_____

_____

_____

III. What to Do with a Conflict of _____

A. If _____ had a conflict of wills, you will too.

B. Let God change your will through _____.

IV. Develop a _____ Team in Decision-Making

PROVERBS 15:22

22 *Without counsel purposes are disappointed: but in the multitude of counsellors they are established.*

PROVERBS 24:6

6 *For by wise counsel thou shalt make thy war: and in multitude of counsellors there is safety.*

PSALM 119:24

24 *Thy testimonies also are my delight and my counsellors.*

PROVERBS 11:14

14 *Where no counsel is, the people fall: but in the multitude of counsellors there is safety.*

Conclusion

_____

_____

_____

Study Questions

1. Read Genesis 24 and list four truths God teaches you about His leading.

2. What does Genesis 24 also teach us about true love?

3. Are you listening to God and looking for His leading right now? What is He trying to tell you through the circumstances you are facing?

4. Describe what a strong decision and what a weak decision would look like. What makes a decision strong?

5. It is important that you not let a conflict of wills with God become what?

6. How should you resolve a conflict of wills with God?

7. Look up what God says in Proverbs about counsel and write out two of those verses.

8. List the godly people to whom you will go for biblical counsel. (This is your team of advisors.)

Memory Verse

"I will instruct thee and teach thee in the way which thou shalt go: I will guide thee with mine eye."—PSALMS 32:8

A Passion to Finish My Course
Embracing Patient Endurance

Text

2 TIMOTHY 4:5–7

5   *But watch thou in all things, endure afflictions, do the work of an evangelist, make full proof of thy ministry.*
6   *For I am now ready to be offered, and the time of my departure is at hand.*
7   *I have fought a good fight, I have finished my course, I have kept the faith:*

Overview

This lesson introduces the third and final passion of biblical adulthood—a passion to finish my course. Our culture is wired for immediate gratification. We view life as a sprint rather than a marathon, and this lesson is designed to build endurance and long-term perspective into the students. The best blessings and experiences in God's will take time, and these principles will equip the students to be steadfast in a world that pressures them to take the easy route.

The lesson includes four principles—patience, contentment, confidence, renewal. These are values that will keep us running when we're doubting, weary, and facing trials in God's will.

Lesson Aim

To help the students patiently engage in the marathon of the Christian life, endure through tests, and finish strong for the Lord.

Introduction

_____

_____

I. Finishing Your Course Requires _____

_____

_____

II. Finishing Your Course Requires _____

_____

_____

III. Finishing Your Course Requires Enduring _____

_____

_____

IV. Finishing Your Course Requires _____

_____

_____

Conclusion

_____

_____

Study Questions

1. Define patience as used often in the Bible.

2. Write out Hebrews 10:36.

3. What are you most impatient about in your life right now?

4. Define contentment from God's Word.

5. What in life are you most wanting right now? How does this "want" impact your relationship with God?

6. Write out 2 Corinthians 4:7–9.

7. Define confidence as used in the Bible.

8. List three things you can do this week to bring renewal to your soul.

Memory Verses

"Blessed is the man that walketh not in the counsel of the ungodly, nor standeth in the way of sinners, nor sitteth in the seat of the scornful. But his delight is in the law of the Lord; and in his law doth he meditate day and night. And he shall be like a tree planted by the rivers of water, that bringeth forth his fruit in his season; his leaf also shall not wither; and whatsoever he doeth shall prosper."—Psalm 1:1–3

The Best Life
Choosing the Path of Most Resistance

Text

2 CHRONICLES 16:9

9 For the eyes of the LORD run to and fro throughout the whole earth, to shew himself strong in the behalf of them whose heart is perfect toward him.

Overview

This lesson reviews the whole study in three main points and wraps up with a final challenge to embrace God's will with passion and commitment.

Be prepared to share decisions you have made, principles you have learned, and how your life has been impacted. Finish the study with a season of prayer together, asking God to solidify the truth in each heart.

Lesson Aim

To review the entire *Life Quest* study and challenge each student to fully embrace God's will for their lives with passion and commitment.

Introduction

_____

_____

_____

I. What's _____ Us Back

_____

_____

_____

II. What's _____ For Us

_____

_____

_____

III. Getting from _____ to _____

_____

_____

_____

Conclusion

_____

_____

_____

Study Questions

1. Looking back on this study, what are the biggest principles God has taught you?

2. Of the things that hold us back, which one are you most susceptible to?

3. List the three wonderful rewards of pursuing God with passion.

4. Write out Nahum 1:7.

5. What big three passions must be in place in your life as you press forward?

6. Of these three passions, which one do you most need to grow in?

7. List three decisions you will make today as a result of this study.

8. Take a moment in prayer and commit to the Lord regarding the things you just listed.

Memory Verse

"The LORD is good, a strong hold in the day of trouble; and he knoweth them that trust in him."—NAHUM 1:7

Striving Together
P u b l i c a t i o n s

For additional Christian
growth resources visit
www.strivingtogether.com